The University of Hip-Hop

THE DRINKING GOURD CHAPBOOK POETRY PRIZE

SERIES EDITORS

Chris Abani

John Alba Cutler

Reginald Gibbons

Susannah Young-ah Gottlieb

Ed Roberson

Matthew Shenoda

The University of Hip-Hop

Poems

Mayda Del Valle

NORTHWESTERN UNIVERSITY PRESS

EVANSTON, ILLINOIS

*To my mother, Carmen "Min" Feliciano, to my nieces Isabella and
Olivia, and to the young women who've sat in circle sharing their stories
during Street Poets workshops at Camp Joseph Scott Detention Center*

Northwestern University Press
www.nupress.northwestern.edu

Northwestern University Poetry and Poetics Colloquium
poetry.northwestern.edu

Printed in the United States of America

10 9 8 7 6 5 4 3 2

Library of Congress Cataloging-in-Publication Data
Names: Valle, Mayda Del, author.
Title: The university of hip-hop : poems / Mayda Del Valle.
Other titles: Drinking gourd chapbook poetry prize.
Description: Evanston, Illinois : Northwestern University Press, 2017. |
Series: The drinking gourd chapbook poetry prize
Identifiers: LCCN 2016044893 | ISBN 9780810135093 (pbk. : alk. paper)
Subjects: LCSH: Chicago (Ill.)—Poetry.
Classification: LCC PS3622.A52524 U55 2017 | DDC 811.6—dc23
LC record available at https://lccn.loc.gov/2016044893

Contents

Foreword

Chris Abani

In the mid-1990s on the South Side of Chicago, an innovative arts and youth advocacy group called the Southwest Youth Collaborative—with an unusual board of equal adult and youth representation—launched a summer program devised by the young beneficiaries called the University of Hip-Hop. One of those beneficiaries and young leaders was Mayda Del Valle. The University of Hip-Hop was built around the four elements of hip-hop: emceeing, which we think of as rap; b-boying, which is dance; graffiti, which covers the visual arts; and DJing, which spans composition and change—all integral parts of a dynamic aesthetic movement.

The aims of this summer program (aside from being an after-school program) were to facilitate the development of different forms of artistic expression in collaboration and community, to redirect energies from possible mischief into creativity, and to educate young people on how hip-hop was a youth-driven movement that could be used as an organizing tool. Elements of this thinking about hip-hop, young people, and organizing were deployed by the early Obama campaign, which targeted young people by using graphics such as the iconic Obama "Change" poster; it is still employed in Ferguson and other scenes of the Black Lives Matter movement. I am not saying that the University of Hip-Hop was directly responsible for any of this, but it was an early marker of a still-current zeitgeist.

Hip-hop has close ties to the spoken-word movement, offering a way for communities of marginalized youth to give voice to protest while also articulating self-identity in response to imposed societal definitions. Hip-hop is an art form that allows for the narration of ignored histories, both personal and public, employing long poetic forms. These elements are present in this chapbook collection, where the long-form poems cover everything from family, identity, place (in many ways this entire collection is a love letter to Chicago), and love, to the more political notions of gender, race, and nation.

By virtue of its performativity, spoken word has flirted dangerously with access, surprising readers and listeners with unexpected slant rhymes, colloquial turns of phrase juxtaposed at seeming odds with one another, and even occasional dips into cliché. All of these are aimed at establishing a larger conversation with a more varied audience than lyric poetry attracts. This risk is something that all fans of Larry Levis will understand: the delicate and precise skill of leaning up against, but never spilling into, sentimentality.

Bomba, salsa, and other Latin- and West African–inspired elements texture this collection. One such tradition, carried over from Africa and the Caribbean, is that of libation or invocation. Even contemporary hip-hop culture, informed by street culture, has the libation for fallen comrades. When Del Valle places "Call Water, Call Agua," a poem of invocation, at the opening of the book, she squarely sets it into that tradition.

In the world of hip-hop performance, DJs are like the conductors of a classical recital. They set the tone of the event, curate a set, and chart a path through. Here Del Valle uses this Delphic, oracular move in "Chicago, c. 1993: Mix Tape as Ars Poetica," enacting it as a DJ set, teaching us how to read this book—showing us where the breaks are, where the variation might be, where the innovation comes in, and where the familiar is being struck. From the first poem to the last, we are in the thrall of a performance curated and directed by Mayda Del Valle. It is notoriously difficult to transfer the three-dimensionality and immediacy of performance to the two-dimensional space of a book. The poet manages the collection by curating it so that the reader can DJ the poems, arrange their own set, and thus, to borrow a phrase from the world of hip-hop, "spin" their own performance.

I invite you into this book to play.

Call Water, Call Agua

spill omi to call agua
spill omi to call iya agua

rock the body
let the shoulders undulate rain
like movement made in mourning

feet pound drum beat
white flowers watermelon molasses
seashells hold her sound
starfish gaze
deep her night and morning

whisper of wet
fog foam drops
grows into her roar tides
moves ache out the heart
washes hurt from the chest
past off the hands
moves calm into her belly
cleans clear crystalline
omi agua water

head fills with wet
head fills with omi
head rocks   shoulders
chest and legs move
like omi

let hands call
let feet spell
let mouths call

      omi oooooooooo
      omi ooooooooooO

mami spread your skirt
omi agua water
over the parch of this concrete angel
fill the cienegas and canyons
green again

      omi ooooooooooo
      omi ooooooooooo

iya carry us home
omi agua water
back to ourselves
across the seas
held precious
in the shelter of your palm

water to call
we call
water to call
we call

the mother of fish
water we call
iya
the madre of clouds
water we call
iya
the madre who washes the path
iya who feeds humankind
madre connecting the continents
madre protecting our crossing
iya who yields the rain sword

2

madre who wears the silver crown
iya who beholds her beauty in the mirror
iya who lives deep in omi
mother who fills all the dry spaces
mother who moistens what we've hidden
iya who heals
madre renews
madre who heals
iya who holds
iya protects

iya mother madre
     omi ooooooooooo
     omi ooooooooooo

water to call water
we call water
water to call water
we call
iya mother madre
we call water
iya mother madre

                  we call water

Chicago, c. 1993
Mix Tape as Ars Poetica

back in the days
when i was young i'm not a kid anymore
but some days
i sit and wish i was a kid again

—Ahmad

Original Mix:

We'd roll together me and my people
always together
tight-knit like wool sweaters
with dreams of making it
big in our city—or making our city big.

Squeezed into the back of an '86 light blue hooptie
Honda Civic whose bumper we'd sometimes retrieve
a block or two behind us—still

The kicker box stuffed into the back trunk
bumping *Illmatic* and *Ready to Die*
made us feel like we was the shit.

On our way to see Common, live,
before he lost the sense,
we'd roll northward—kings and queens of Chicago's South Side planet
'cause anyone who's ever been there knows
it's a whole other world.

Cut:

People drive past us on Lake Shore Drive
witness to the antics of teens
who've discovered that weed makes weekends
with difficult parents easier to stomach.

Their scowling brows take in the pants sliding off our asses
oversized T-shirts clinging to our shoulders
staring at us like   outer space
reminding us
        You're lucky you get to go out at all. When I was your age . . .

We wave off their admonishments
make out in the back seat while friends drive us to the mall
later hiding hickeys with turtlenecks
or trying to twist them off with a cold lipstick top.

Cut:

Spray can in one hand bottle of cheap liquor in the other
backpacks and fat laces
we swore we'd rep the Chi for life
carry the rhythm of fat caps, funk, skateboards, and turntables.

I pull my skully with the brim low
pull up my men's size 32 jeans
and bob my head to this, my era of hip-hop.

Break:

I reminisce on the cipher of familiar faces.

Rewind:

Hitting up the corner store
we trade our Saturday nights and fake ID's
for bags of Swedish Fish and Cool Ranch Doritos
buying cheap bottles of Boones and margarita mix.
We gather every weekend to let the smoke
of hand-rolled jays wander across our faces
like clouds across our city's skyline
during summer thunderstorms.

We gather in that cipher
six or seven deep with a deep-dish
pizza from Palermo's
a twelve-pack of icy RC colas
and watch *Style Wars* or *Beat Street*
dreaming we'd travel to New York
bomb train yards like it was still back in the day.

Remix:

We were so new school,
worshipping anything
that anchored our devotion
to hip-hop in authenticity.
We were in love
with a culture that gave us the space
to rebel against our parents' blue-collar dreams.
In love with music that gave us reason.

After a few rounds of passing the jay
and once the *Style Wars* tape starts

to rewind itself in the VCR
we roll
downtown into the Loop
with nothing but the clothes we racked from Marshall's,
the paint we'd racked from the True Value,
and the names we picked—

Scratch:

meela	peas	side 2	actor
bigs	noble	vegas	sam one
sleek			

Cut:

We sneak into subway tunnels,
slink like rats that claim the underground,
and emerge
with paint-dripped shell toes,
cold noses, and fingers
turned aqua black and pink

run the El tracks
suspended above the below-
zero streets of Chicago
wishing we were suspended in time.

Blessed with the cockiness of being sixteen
we believed we ran the city.

Scratch:

Before the broken hearts
before the reality of bills and student loans
before the reality of Infamil and Pampers
before the now and later sweetness of our youth
we existed within that cipher of familiar faces
with hip-hop as our soundtrack
and fear never factored into our futures

'cause—

Time Line

1978
Latex can fail.

1979
Carter.

1980
Red flowers, white dress. Buster Browns. Screen windows. Bangs. Lace socks. That lady who always sings too loud and nasally at church.

1981
St. Basil. Easter Mass. Handmade dresses and bonnets. Frankincense gold chain swing, red and white altar boys, cheeks poked like ripe avocados.

1982
A-E-I-O-U and sometimes Y. The Cuban neighbor's husky Natasha has one blue and one green eye.

1983
Bowl cut. Corduroy overalls. Christmas pageant school gym. Big brother white navy hat and uniform visits.

1984
White people everywhere. Priests' tongue foreign. New nuns school.

1985
Sorry Jesus for talking in class. Wood planks leave lines in knees. Shame feels like a bowl of hot soup in your belly.

1986
Snow white lily winter day. A closet tastes inappropriate in her mouth.

1987
Rice Krispie treats, bake-sale cookies.

1988
Perms smell crazy.

1989
Berlin. No Saturday morning cartoons.

1990
Ibuprofen alleviates abdominal pain.

1991
First kiss: way sloppier than I thought.

1992
Maria High School. Bigger buildings. Room numbers. New uniforms.

1993
The bathroom is the perfect place to hide from boys who ask me to
dance.

1994
Ready to Die. Illmatic. Gin and Juice. Bomb the Suburbs. 36 Chambers.
A smoke-filled '84 Honda Civic.

1995
A small red bloom gives me a shit-eating grin at Thanksgiving dinner.

1996
Lots of white people. Again. Ivy-covered buildings. Count brown
faces and miles from home. Stubborn refusal to call a cramped
dorm room *home*.

1997

The city starts to slip off the tongue but the academy does not find footing on the palate.

1998

Prodigal daughter island humidity return. Old women recognize the mother written on the face and in the smile.

1999

Africa. Durban. First sunburn below the equator. More brown faces than I have ever seen.

2000

Caps and gowns. New city home. Chino-Latino restaurants. Spanish Harlem. Subways that run all day and night. Apple martinis. The Nuyoricans' creaky floor. Poems. Words. Microphones. Hosts. Lists. The first rent check.

2001

House fire. Everything covered in soot. Furniture, books, clothes. Nothing turned to ash. Just soot. No security deposit returned.

2002

Poems. Poems. Poems. Delivered in a dark Broadway theater. Rita Moreno stood right here.

2003

The grind. One day off a week. Eight shows a week. Sore throats. Poems. Bronchitis. Poems. Fever. Poems. Pulled muscles. Poems. Delivered in a dark theater.

2004

Tour. A new city every day. Every week. A suitcase carries home. Hotel rooms all smell the same. Unless it's a five-star. ORD has the best bathrooms.

2005
A new city.
A new lease.
A clichéd lover.
An old story.

2006
L.A. L.A. No seasons.
All sun all day.
The dead visit my dreams in L.A.

2007
Heineken changes the tone of his voice.

2008
That damn rent check.

2009
A decade later. Island return on my terms. Santurce sunrise.
La Respuesta on Monday nights.
B-boys Boricua style. Medallas and chichaitos.

2010
2nd island return on my terms.
Consider this: 85 degrees every day. Beach every day.
Leave behind another clichéd lover and make the floating rock home?

2011
L.A. The solitude is startling.

2012
This lover considers buying me an emerald ring.
Small hands small fingers.

This Is How You Leave Home

I want to ask you if you ever wanted to leave.
If you can see yourself living somewhere other than here:
this city that put the wind in your lungs,
the ice in your stare.

It's not that I hated home—
it's just that my sense of destiny made me look
beyond the invisible border.

The night before I left for college,
my cousin Edgar married his high school sweetheart Rocio.
The coral dresses my sister and I wore were just like
the ones we wore a week earlier for her best friend Delilah's wedding.
My mother wished we just recycled those damn dresses—
no one would have known the difference.

Rocio's youngest brother looked at me all night
like he wished we'd met sooner
and when I saw him a year later on a trip home
when my sister was dating his older brother
his gaze slipped up and down the extra freshman fifteen
that had settled in places that bordered on adolescent
the last time he saw me.

Anyway—

we left the reception early, came back to the house to finish packing.
Already in the back seat were the green Samsonite
suitcases we used for that trip to Puerto Rico when I was five,
boxes with my twin-sized bedding, my favorite stuffed animal
jammed up next to the dorm-room-sized fridge and small TV
with built-in VCR that they got me from Service Merchandise.

I took off the coral taffeta, looked around the wreck of my room:
the white canopy frame that I'd slept under since I was three,
taken apart and put downstairs, so I could leave the mattress
on the floor, attempt to have a grown-looking room.

That was the last summer, the last time I ran up to the sweltering cathedral
cavern of our attic, swung out the windows so I could stick my head out,
just to catch a glimpse of downtown, far out in the distance.
I could see the sparkling outline of the Sears Tower and the
    John Hancock.

When we got on the I-90 heading east to Indiana I looked back
to see the point of the Sears Tower blink in the distance.
Repeating my mother's exodus from her island birthplace
to escape from her mother. I inherit this tendency to run.
On the radio: *This is how we chill from '93 till.*

This Is How Our Bodies Are Made to Apologize

I was the girl who worked behind the counter at the skate shop. Never stepped on a skateboard, but could put one together like one of the boys. Grip tape, German ball bearings, Indy wheels, and Shorty hardware with a grip tape cut so clean the corner barber woulda looked twice. It was just me and him on the morning and afternoon shift. I wore thin worn polo shirts I bought at the thrift store, 'cause the vintage polyester hung different, and thin white cotton bras that I didn't know didn't always hide the dark outline of my areolas. I had my hat on backwards. My men's size 33 Girbauds hung just right on my ass and my black-and-white Airwalks had just got a new pair of extra-wide fat laces. He approached me from down the counter, walked over to where I was to grab a wrench, and looked down my shirt. *I can see through it*, he said and brushed my breast, and as his hand came back down I cringed and my shoulders shot forward, chest caving in on itself like a rose blooming inward. He stood in front of me, the wall of wrenches and shoelaces and skateboards behind me, and I had nowhere to go.

Being Carmen's Daughter

Primero it's hablando in whatever language
fits your need at the moment.
It's stories about an unbalanced spirit-seeing
grandmother, about crinoline-ruffled slips
covered in Caribbean floral prints.
It's baby daughter to a baby daughter.
It's your best outfit and shoes made
to last more than a decade.
It's becoming a repository of family recipes.
It's laughter louder than everyone else
in the room, ghosts in the corner
speaking of the dead with reverence and wonder.
It's dreams about weddings meaning
death is around the corner.
It's Catholic hymns and rose-scented rosaries.
It's Virgin Mary litanies.
It's food and arthritic hands
pressing milk out ground coconut.
It's clean, it's bleach and mops
and vacuums and no dust and
"I have to go home and clean."
It's "Keep your legs closed,
don't trust anyone not even your own feet."
It's "Don't depend on any man."
It's "I wish I could have's"
that bloom break and bleed
in unfulfilled unheard possibilities.

In the Cocina

mami's makin' mambo
mami's makin' mambo

In the domain of the Del Valle kitchen my mother is the dictator.
I refer to it as "Carmen's culinary queendom."
She becomes a cuisine conquistadora
wielding a freshly sharpened knife like a sword above her head.
Here Goya doesn't stand a chance.
No pre-packaged shit.
She is the menu mercenary,
the soldier of soul food.

You need to back the hell up
'cause
 mami's makin' mambo

She hangs the hats of iron chefs off the windowsill like roast-duck trophies
and laughs at the sight of any edible food item

Mua ha ha ha ha ha ha!

No meat in the freezer?
poof!
Spam and corned beef in a can are transformed into virtual filet mignon.
poof!
Rice cooks itself instantly at her command
and beans
jump into bubbling pots shrieking,
"Carmen, please!!! Cook me, master, please! Honor me with your spice!"
    Emeril and Julia Child
    mere hamburger flippers in her presence.

'cause
mami's makin' mambo

It was there
in my mother's kitchen
that I learned more than just how to cook.
It's where I learned the essence of rhythm and power.
I learned to dance in that kitchen.
Shiny aluminum rice pots clanging like cowbells
with metal spoons, cast-iron frying pans,
the wooden mortar and pestle provided the percussion section.
With the radio humming softly in the background
the fall of her steel blade on the wooden cutting board
became the clave. The hissing of the pressure cooker harmonized
with the sizzling of sofrito and bubbling beans softening in covered pots
and her hands moved faster than Mongo's on congas during a riff
making mofongo con caldo.
She would say to me
        The way to a man's heart is through his stomach and your hips.
        So you better learn how to cook, mija.
She gave me the secret recipe for ritmo

2 ½ cups of caderas
a lb. of gyrating pelvis
a pinch of pursed lips
a tb. of shaking shoulders
and a generous helping of *soooooouuul.*
Combine and mix.
        This is the recipe for ritmo, and now
        I'm dancing the way my mother cooks

Slow
Sultry spicy
Sabrosa
Natural

Instinctively
Drippin' sweet sweat like fresh leche de coco
Spinnin' as fast as piraguas melt in summertime South Side heat
Dancin' with as much kick as cuchifrito and Bacardi
Standin' strong like a morning-time Bustelo
Steamy as pasteles at Christmas
Blendin' my hip-hop y mambo like a piña-colada
my mouth watering for music
with sabor en caderas
soothes down my hips
dulce as Celia's
Azzúcarr
Con dulzura
I'm cooking with sabor
I'm bailando con sabor
'cause

mami's makin' mambo
mami's makin' mambo

> *Mamucha. Come eat.*
> *The food's ready.*

Why You Talk Like That?
Or, The Etymology of "Where Are You Really From?"

'cause it's a language of necessity
'cause it's translating for my father at the social security office
and my mother having a reader's digest subscription for over 30 years
'cause i grew up on 64th and california
'cause i went to an ivy league and clutched
onto the south side
the way a hawk grasps its prey
hunting the hood in my dialect every time
i came back home and the homies said
you sound white
right now
like
you not from here
no more

'cause you're so regional
you sound so chicago
and you speak english so well
how did you learn
'cause folks know i'm from where i'm from
when i say shit like pop
and drawl the caw
in chicago
'cause i got a lineage
of brujas sing-songin'
their black cat
callin' conjurations caught on my incisors
'cause i code-switch between magic and academic
'cause i coño carajo me cago en na'
feel like it
'cause oakland gave me hella even tho i never lived there

'cause que
porque
qué pasó
qué hace
nada
quién eres
'cause the world thinks i'm nada
thinks brown girls are nada
nadie
nobody think they gotta listen
so i extra lip smack
away the silence
with a head swing in spanglish
and muthafucka
fuck fuck
fania salsa
slip my way across this bridge i live on

This Is How the City Began to Slip

I think this story is only for those who know what they leave.

The way my mother talks about leaving PR at 17:
how all her memories are soft-focus vignettes,
chirping birds, blooming tropical flowers, sunsets
and the light strains of a guitar strumming jibaro music
on some Boricua Disney princess type of shit.

The way her memory defies the reality of the island now:
bass-heavy reggaeton rattling,
highways surgically slicing into mountainsides,
polluted rivers, gruesome murders,
and men with shaved eyebrows.

I left Chicago eighteen years ago;
gone the same amount of time I lived there.
All I have are soft-focus vignettes of a 17-year-old girl
The city I left doesn't exist anymore either.
More mythic than anything else, I dress her in memory,
the city veiled in nostalgia.

The boys I liked are married with children.
The train lines we used as playgrounds
barricaded behind security cameras.
Sears Tower is Willis,
Comiskey now Cellular Field,
Gertie's on 59th a cell phone store:
Chicago is a corporation.

Our neighbors of ten years are getting foreclosed on.
Mad houses sit empty and shuttered on my folks' block
red brick bungalows staring into the winter snow mud.

My mother prays every day to get the fuck out too.
Every doubled tripled quadrupled utility bill
strains their Social Security pension income.
Every winter seems colder than the last,
every inch of skin seems thinner against the ice.

But I always come back like a prodigal daughter,
sometimes feeling like I'm not from here,
some days thinking it's the only place that could ever be home,
the only place that knows me.

Ode to Door-Knocker Earrings

all golden and round
the way girl
all bent
metal circular crown
of flash
me queen
dangling from aural
bass boom receivers.
all hood
honeydrop hoops.

oh precious metal display of ego!
oh golden calf circumference
of *chingona* chola confidence!
oh amulet incantation of my name
set in malleable metallurgical mix
of alloy alchemy.

i don't think they did my name in 14k

but fuck it,

i steady rock
the tarnish anyway
anywhere.

when i meet my creator
dress me in fat laces
a bandera de Lares
and my downtown L.A.
swap meet gold
weighed in ounces.

yea i rock the name my mama gave me on my ear.
yea i wore a white tux and gold bamboos
to shake the president's hand.
and what?

gilded ghetto regalia
ladies first
regal steeze
B-girl couture
Louis Vuitton please.

the bigger the hoop
the bigger the—
the bigger the—
call me out my name

say my name
say my name
those that can't say my name
it's on my earring B
just read it

all gold all gold
all precious mineral
on precious skin body
adornment no delicate dainty
these my royal jewels.

Chronology of Sound

Jan. 14

The echoes of water drops falling into the tub and I'm alone in the bath-
room
    reverb off the walls.

Jan. 15

9:14 A.M. The sound of planes over the apartment getting washed out by
traffic.

Jan. 16

The crows at 8 A.M. Caws.
Black shadows crossing overhead just outside the curtains.

Jan. 18

Dana's voice singing for Orixa over drums
    Orin nee ya nee ya
    harmonize her angel tone I have to stop and listen.

Jan. 19

The hum of the air coming through the vents
    hhhhhhhhhhh.

Jan. 20

The flutter of pages on my desk when the heat moves them,
a ruffle of paper.

Jan. 21

The exhale of the heating system when the air turns off.

Jan. 22

The hiss the skin of my foot makes when it slides across the metal chair.

Jan. 23

The keys of my laptop make a different sound without the vinyl cover. More click and scratch with the nails.

Jan. 24

The breath coming out his nose when he wakes up and smiles in the morning. The sound of smiling: *mmm*.

Jan. 25

Maraca shake
makes the sound of rain in my hand.

Jan. 26

The car door closes and I walk back to my car mumbling to myself. Will "I love you's" be said when the doors open?

Jan. 27

The ringtone is called jungle drums.
It's an electronic samba that whistles and
e e e e-e. e e e
when he calls.

Jan. 29

If a smile made a sound it would be 17 yrs old
red velvet chocolate cake happy birthday songs.

Jan. 30

He *mmm*'s and *yea*'s
cuts and edits measures of music.
I can't hear
what's going through his headphones
I fall asleep on the couch to the lullaby of his humming and *yeeeea*.

Feb. 1

There is a close-up picture of our hands together someone has posted
online:
his hands hold a calabash and mine.
Shells sprinkle and clink through my fingers,
spreading them across the shrine.
I flick a lighter and place the flame under a few leaves of sage
that smoke and clear.

Feb. 2

Yemanja Festival

1: When spirit enters
the music enters the ears.
Fills, amplifies.
My hands over my ears do not drown out
the drums' increasing boom,
the vibrations coming up through the floor.
My feet throb. The heat travels up my spine and I think I'm moaning
through the hands.
The voices asking if I'm OK
are far-away echoes on a phone line.

2: The rain is a quiet sigh.

Feb. 3

My back is sore and the only thing I wish I could hear right now is the
bathtub filling.

Feb. 4

6:30 A.M. The fairy bells of the alarm on my phone actually work today
and I get up to write.

Feb. 5

9:45 P.M. Mike the bartender at Alibi. The perfect old-fashioned. Wu-Tang over the speakers is a welcome break from the folk music that was playing when I walked in.

Feb. 7

The days I don't hear his voice, the only sound that stands out to me is his voice. Even my fingers sliding across the screen to check the phone don't make a sound.

Feb. 8

me curé / me curé / con la bomba me curé . . .
1:28 A.M. I fall asleep in the car for a few minutes and wake up to the muffled sound of drums coming through the windows. When I open the door I hear the slap *pra pra pra* of the primo. I play and sing for an hour, wake up enough to drive home with the radio blaring the whole way.

Feb. 9

1: I don't hear his voice today, and despite the traffic, the neighbors playing cumbias, John's heavy zombie footsteps coming up the stairs outside the living room, the house seems extra quiet.

2: Talia's giggle when I flurburt her neck and toss her in the air is magic. Jay's dad clicks camera shots. Sepna says *ohmigod she really loves you.*

Feb. 10

He left a message. The heavy in his voice when I listened to it at 6:27 P.M. made me cut across the freeway and head westside.

Feb. 11

No classes today.

It's been a week and the pain in my shoulder shot down my arm last night like a hot knife. I think it has a sizzling sound.

I called at 10:45 A.M. to let him know I was dropping off the keys. We went to breakfast.

The clink of metal on glass when I stir in the sugar.

His voice is porcelain plates bumping each other at the table when he asks how I know for certain I won't end up sleeping with the ex again.

My voice cracks with offense. I know. How do you know you won't hook up with the Japanese lover again?

Feb. 12

1: Went to see Freyda today. My back cracked top to bottom zipper when she pushed between my shoulders. She whooshes and breathes and pushes and urges me to let the sob out. I'm so tired of all this crying.

2: The mourning doves are back! I heard the whistle of their wings and those sad, sad cries when they were settling into their nest.

Feb. 13

All hotel rooms have the same smell. The same clicking doors. The same beeping elevators. The same heaters/air conditioners clack rattle breathe into the room all night.

Feb. 14

1: The plane engines whir louder upon landing. A rush of mechanical hums and rattling plastic.

2: Wine bottle cork pop. Paper tearing on the gift I got you.

Feb. 15

I gifted him a keyboard for his iPad last night. Subtle clicks while the sheets swish around us. A Skype call rings out, fills the room with the ex-lover from Japan. A sarcastic Happy Valentine's Day fell out my mouth.

Feb. 16

The phone hasn't vibrated with jungle drums today. Fuck. I miss the sound of that ringtone.

Feb. 17

If the burning in my shoulder and neck made a sound it would be the color of red wine. It got worse after the last appointment. Freyda will probably crack the shit out my back this Wednesday though.

Feb. 18

I wish there was an alarm that announced the arrival of the cloud. I can feel it coming over me, but I never hear it approaching.

Feb. 19

The pain has crawled over my shoulder and into the area right above my heart. I keep listening for the pops in my neck that might bring some relief but they don't come.

Feb. 20

Sometimes I wonder if the neighbors can hear me crying. The walls are so thin I have to bury my face into two pillows so I can have a good unself-conscious cry. I'm optimistic though. I don't ever hear people having sex in the neighboring apartments. So either they're soundproof or no one's fucking.

Feb. 21

Today at Locke Eric reads his poem really fast in a nervous voice. The line that stands out: *Just accept the fact that myself is what I have to adore.* I tell him to take a deep breath and read it again. Slowly this time.

Feb. 22

1: M has a -*th* lisp when he has to say an *S*.

2: The kids scratching on their notebooks, while a drum workshop permeates the glass windows along with the sunlight.

3: C came by with Sushi, who jumped from the couch to the sofa for three hours with a rubber toy he chewed to bits. His little face smacks and huffs then spits out the green plastic on my brown rug.

4: 1:15 A.M. *I'm finally home* he texted when my phone chimed.

Feb. 23

Three hours. The ex's voice droned on the phone about himself for almost three hours when I was the one who needed someone to talk to. How the hell did I . . .
When I finally hung up the silence was a relief.
Now I know why that shit didn't work.

Feb. 24

1: 7:30 A.M. I am so drained I can't pull myself out of the bed. The sound of the teakettle doesn't motivate me. Nothing does. The alarm gets snoozed.

2: 8:17 A.M. For the last I-don't-know-how-many years, an unidentified neighbor hawks up half a lung every morning at around the same time while a shower is running somewhere. I can hear it across the entire apartment whether I close the fucking windows or not.

3: 2:14 P.M. I cry to sleep on the couch. I hate the silence right now.

Feb. 25

Everyone was so tired in class tonight. You could hear it in their voices. That kind of monotone drone and stumbling over simple syllables. During workshop there were so few responses the unspoken *I don't give a shit* filled the room like cigarette smoke.

Feb. 26

1: 8:00 A.M. There is a peace in Baba's shrine room that comes from the colors of all the different altars and the music he was playing on the radio.
Salsa songs he found that were all about Orisha.
His block is so quiet. No traffic. No blaring speakers.
When Baba tosses the shells back and forth in his hand, they have a hollow rattle. A kind of wooden shell and the sound ends with conviction when they hit the floor.

The gold bell he rings while he prays always pierces my ear.
When Irete-Ogunda came up as one of my odu's he let out a high-pitched "HA!" that was part surprise and part "I knew there was something up here."
2: The plastic wrapper on the Thin Mint Girl Scout cookies.

Feb. 27

1: The neighbor who practices keyboard and sings rancheras and Mexican pop songs every morning at about 9. I don't know if it's the same one that hawks and *huuuccgggkgkgkgkgkgkgk*

2: 12:48 A.M. The sound of rejection filling my ears. Again. Fuck.
This is the most tired song whose record I can't seem to fucking change.
I can't _____ (fill in the blank) has got to be the shittiest phrase to start any sentence with.
I made tea in the magic tea maker and it always sounds like piss when I put it over the teapot to drain after it's done steeping.
When my voice cracked while I was once again pouring my heart out I took a sip to keep the tears at bay.
His silence filled the room.

Feb. 28

1: 7:30 A.M. It's been raining all night and the gutter outside my window slapping water into the puddle that forms in the dirt is the most welcome sound I've heard in months. But I worry about the mourning doves and if they can keep the nest dry.

2: 9:13 A.M. My neck cracked and I think last night's conversation might have helped.

3: 12 P.M. The wheels of my luggage grinding on the paved walkway.

I made it through most of the day without crying. During my connection in Charlotte, Ashley called me and I was sniffling so loud telling her what happened the guy in the seat next to me kept looking over. I could only turn my face to hide. I kept hearing the patter of the tears from my left eye hitting the vinyl on the chair. I didn't have anything to wipe it up with.

March 1

1:03 A.M. I've had the heater on eighty-six since last night and it's definitely not that warm in the room. It's the one thing about hotel rooms that drives me crazy. There's never a moment without that white noise. And it clicks every few seconds I think when the thermostat checks in.

March 2

The phone rings and chimes over and over.
The people in the airport sideways-glance at my raised voice.
Ten angry text messages in a row.

March 5

I hate my phone and the way it clocks in ex-boyfriend jealousy and bullshit with every ring.

March 6

The silence of my phone is a welcome space. Homegirls call to check in on me. The lilt of a girlfriend's voice brings comfort.

March 9

Does numb have a sound?

March 12

Not even the sound of drums cheers me up today. They *gun-pra gun-pra* annoyance into my ears.

March 14

1: 8 P.M. Beau is a force of nature. His arms wave red and loud. His hands knife the air on the razor edge of each word.

2: 11 P.M. The post-open-mic crew from work comes over for drinks. They fall out listening to Walter Mercado astrology predictions in Spanish. Even with all the Botox, sacred beads, and wide-eyed wonder his astrology reading is on point.

Escorpión! Coje tu tiempo que el amor vendrá a ti. Tienes que conocer la persona, tener una amistad primero. Así el amor sale bien.

March 17

1: 8 A.M. Baba's room is peaceful. His pots and shrines hum what we ask for. I ask about the recently departed lover.

Supposed to be together,

The fuck does that mean?

Peace and victory.

They can't possibly be talking about the same man.

2: 9 P.M. Darkness is a man's voice speaking of rape. It circles in and through the twenty people in the room but settles in the bodies of the three women present.

March 19

Freyda says I'm standing up for myself. And that's a good thing. Being clear about boundaries.

No no no no no no no no no no no.

A sound women are too unfamiliar with.

March 21

Shitty sounds like your car trembling on the freeway.
Shitty sounds like the recently departed lover you are speaking to on the phone while your car is trembling telling you your ex is telling people you've been "hooking up" with someone new.
Shitty sounds like your recently departed lover listening to you laugh as your car overheats and dies on the freeway exit.
Shitty sounds like calling AAA to tow your car two blocks away to the mechanic you were trying to make it to.
Shitty sounds like the mechanic telling you it's going to be at least $2,500 to fix your car.
Shitty sounds like the recently departed lover offering to pick you up and take you home but not calling back until ten-thirty at night.
Grateful sounds like your best friend calling you at seven and saying *Congratulations, let's have a drink! You're getting a new car!*

March 23

Car shopping was not what I'd planned to do with my spring break. I start to feel a sense of panic with every jagged breath throughout the day.

March 24

1: I hate shopping. I hate cars. I hate slimy car salesmen. Every car salesman I've ever dealt with asks me out for a drink. I say thank you for the ride back from the dealership and close the car door. At least the one at Honda is nice.
2: A five-and-a-half-hour staff meeting. It takes four hours for anyone to actually sound completely honest.

March 25

Car shopping day four. My phone is ringing with ten different dealerships and insurance companies.
Exhausted sounds like snoring myself awake on the couch.

March 26

Congratulations on the purchase of your new Honda!

March 27

The recently departed lover hasn't called since I was stranded with no car. I finger the steering wheel of my new ride. The volume on the radio only goes up to forty. Bronx River Parkway sounds awesome on the new speakers anyway. There's no more bass rattle of a busted speaker from the back seat.

March 29

Today is the first day I sit down and write. The scribble of my pen on paper is a welcome sound. Overwhelmed sounds like a sandbag being dropped on your chest.

April 1

The recently departed lover calls at midnight. You're in Tampa and half asleep. The jungle drum ring tone doesn't sound since you've deleted all his information so you answer it accidentally. It's been ten days since the car died and now he calls to ask how you're doing. Did everything work out with it? Oh the other thing I was calling for is to see if you know of a poem or do you have a poem that I could use for this project and song I was working on honoring women.
This is definitely what a bad joke sounds like.

April 4

Tonight we had 99% women at the open mic. An eight-year-old got up and read a piece about magic and dragons. That's the sound of poetic justice.
I sang one of my songs and I danced while the recently departed lover played drums.
I left his shirt, book, and CDs on top of his bag without saying a word. We barely spoke.

11:45 P.M. My phone vibrates in my purse while I listen to an all-female mariachi band. The lead singer is wailing and crying about a lost love. The kind of voice and pitch that makes the hair on the back of your neck stand up.

The recently departed lover texts: *you killed it tonight. you were great.*

April 9

The whir of plane engines doesn't faze me anymore. Wheels up on the red-eye to Durham. At least it's a direct flight.

April 10

Students at East Carolina University are all raucous laughter and questions. There's a poem about women's bodies. A poem about kung fu. There are questions about spirituality and sweat lodges. There is the sound of breathing deep in spite of the sandbag on my chest.

April 13

A car alarm wails for an hour.

Acknowledgments and Shout-Outs

My deepest love and thanks to my mother and father, my siblings, and my nieces and nephew.

Thank you, Cheefee, for your encouragement, your counsel, and for reminding me it was way past time to get this done. I wouldn't have finished this without you. To Hedgebrook, for giving me the time and space to nurture my voice. To Luis Rodríguez, who continues to be a mentor after so many years. To the Nuyorican Poets Café, for existing in this universe.

Eternal gratitude to the Southwest Youth Collaborative—Jeremy Lahoud, Camille Odeh, Jonathan Peck, and Gillian Young-Miller—for the many years you dedicated to the youth of the South Side of Chicago, for believing that we as young people had the power to transform our own lives, to create the city as well as the world anew. You changed my life. To Sandra Burton of the Williams College dance department and Marcela Peacock: you helped me survive the Purple Valley.

Deep appreciation to the judges of the 2016 Drinking Gourd Chapbook Poetry Prize: John Alba Cutler, Reginald Gibbons, Susannah Gottlieb, Ed Roberson, and in particular Chris Abani and Matthew Shenoda for your editorial advice. Thank you for this honor.

Mayda Del Valle is a poet and performer who has been described by the *Chicago Sun-Times* as having "a way with words. Sometimes they seem to flutter and roll off her lips. Other times they burst forth like a comet streaking across a nighttime sky."

A proud native of Chicago's South Side, she appeared on six episodes of *Russell Simmons Def Poetry Jam* on HBO and was a contributing writer and original cast member of the Tony Award–winning *Def Poetry Jam on Broadway*.

She has been featured in *Latina* magazine, *The Source*, and the *New York Times*, and she was named by the *Smithsonian* magazine as one of America's Young Innovators in the Arts and Sciences. *O, The Oprah Magazine* selected her for their first-ever "O Power List" of twenty visionary women making a mark in business, politics, and the arts. In May 2009 she was invited to perform at the White House for President Obama and the First Lady.

Del Valle is currently program director of the poetry-based, nonprofit youth organization Street Poets Inc. and a dancer and vocalist with the Los Angeles–based Afro-Puerto Rican bomba group Cunyá.